# ANCIENT ROME

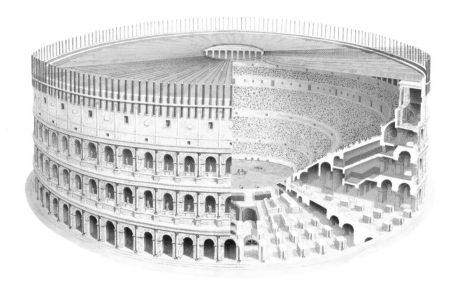

Published in Great Britain in 2003 by
The British Museum Press
A division of The British Museum Company Ltd
46 Bloomsbury Street, London WC1B 3QQ

ISBN 0 7141 3026 5

*Everyday Life in Ancient Rome*
was created and produced by McRae Books
via de' Rustici, 5 – Florence (Italy)
e-mail: info@mcraebooks.com

Series Editor Anne McRae
Text Neil Grant
Illustrations Manuela Cappon, Lorenzo Cecchi, Matteo Chesi,
Ferruccio Cucchiarini, Luisa Della Porta, Sauro Giampaia,
Sabrina Marconi, Paola Ravaglia, Andrea Ricciardi di Gaudesi,
Giacomo Soriani, Studio Stalio (Alessandro Cantucci,
Fabiano Fabbrucci, Andrea Morandi)
Graphic Design Marco Nardi
Layout Laura Ottina, Adriano Nardi
Editing Susan Kelly and Anne McRae
Repro Litocolor, Florence
Picture Research Susan Kelly

Printed and bound in Belgium

**Neil Grant**

# ANCIENT

## EVERYDAY LIFE IN

# ROME

Illustrations by Manuela Cappon, Luisa Della Porta,
Paola Ravaglia, Andrea Ricciardi di Gaudesi, Studio Stalio

THE BRITISH MUSEUM PRESS

# Table of Contents

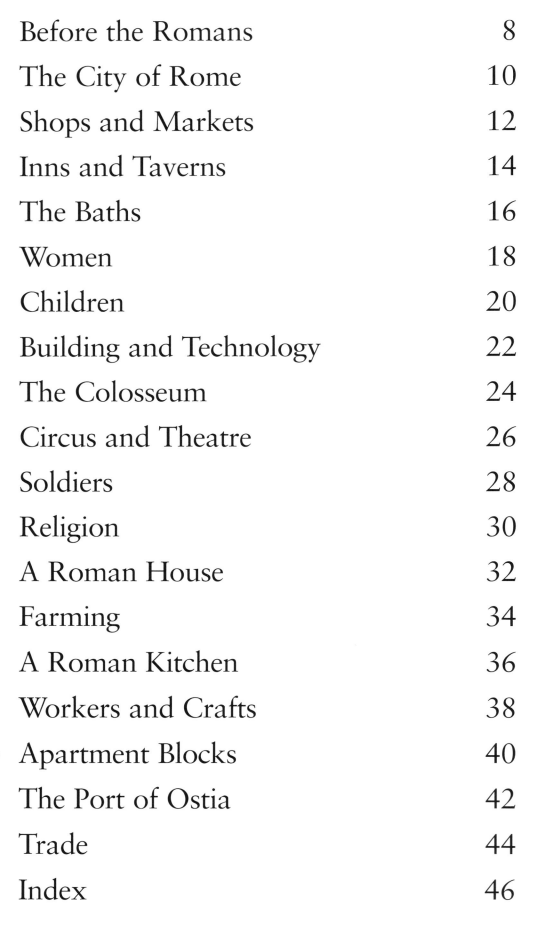

# Introduction

In 753 BC Rome was no more than a few peasants' huts, but it grew to become the centre of a great empire. About 500 BC the Romans threw off Etruscan rule and established a republic. By 300 BC, the Roman Republic dominated Italy, and by 146 BC it had destroyed its chief rivals in the Mediterranean, Carthage and Greece. But while its territory expanded, the Republic was in trouble, with civil war, dictatorship, and rivalry between army leaders. Julius Caesar seized power in 46 BC but was assassinated by men who feared he would make himself king. His adopted son became the first Roman emperor and named himself Augustus. Some early emperors were bad rulers, yet the empire continued to grow. From the late 1st to the 3rd century AD, the 'Roman peace' brought general prosperity to an empire that, by 117, stretched from Scotland to Syria, including north Africa. But by about 150, the empire was on the defensive against envious neighbours. From the 3rd century it began a long decline, and the empire was divided into east and west. The last emperor in the west was finally overthrown in 476. The eastern Byzantine empire continued.

For 1,000 years after the fall of the empire, Roman civilization remained the model for Europeans. The Roman language, Latin, was the common language of educated people until the 16th century. Roman law is the basis of much modern European law even now. The Roman empire was an international civilization. It included people of many races, religions, and languages, who were united under Roman government. The title 'Holy Roman Emperor' was held by some European rulers until 1806. It could even be argued that the European Union is another attempt to regain the unity that the Romans first achieved.

## Chronology of Ancient Rome

|  |  |
|---|---|
| BEGINNINGS OF ETRUSCAN CIVILIZATION | *about 800 BC* |
| MYTHICAL FOUNDATION OF ROME | 753 BC |
| FOUNDATION OF ROMAN REPUBLIC | 509 BC |
| ETRUSCAN CIVILIZATION DECLINES | *from about 400 BC* |
| FIRST PUNIC WAR | 264 BC–241 BC |
| SECOND PUNIC WAR | 218 BC–204 BC |
| THIRD PUNIC WAR | 149–146 BC |
| CONQUEST OF GAUL | 58–51 BC |
| BEGINNING OF IMPERIAL RULE | 27 BC |
| CONQUEST OF BRITAIN | AD 43 |
| ROMAN EMPIRE AT ITS GREATEST EXTENT | AD 116 |
| EMPIRE DIVIDED INTO EAST AND WEST | AD 286 |
| VISIGOTHS SACK ROME | AD 410 |
| VANDALS CAPTURE CARTHAGE | AD 439 |
| VANDALS SACK ROME | AD 455 |
| FALL OF THE WESTERN ROMAN EMPIRE | AD 476 |

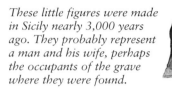

We know very little of the early people of Italy, except through objects, like this metal incense burner, that archaeologists have found in their graves.

These little figures were made in Sicily nearly 3,000 years ago. They probably represent a man and his wife, perhaps the occupants of the grave where they were found.

# Before the Romans

Nearly 3,000 years ago the people of Iron Age Italy belonged to a large number of different tribes. Living in scattered villages, they were farmers and hunters and, by about the 8th century BC, skilful craftspeople too. Around that time, a new, more advanced culture developed in Etruria (Tuscany). These Etruscan people lived in many small city-states, which often fought against each other. Rome was ruled by Etruscan kings until 509 BC, when the last king was driven out and a republic was founded.

## An Iron Age village

The village that became Rome on the Palatine Hill (where the vast palaces of the Roman emperors would one day stand) may have looked like this 3,000 years ago. The people raised crops and animals, and they seem to have been fond of horses as many bits of harness have been found in their graves. Their huts had walls of mud on a frame of sticks, with thatched roofs. The hill site gave some security against attack.

## Etruscans and Greeks

The Etruscans were the most advanced people in Italy before the rise of Rome. They influenced the Romans, and were themselves influenced by the Greeks, who had established colonies in southern Italy. Between 500 and 200 BC the Romans conquered most of Italy, including Etruria and the Greek colonies.

*Sardinia (500 BC)*

*This terracotta head of a goddess was made in Rome by an Etruscan craftsman who had been influenced by Greek art. The mysterious smile was a trademark of early Greek and Etruscan sculptors.*

*This warrior (right) wears an Etruscan helmet with a typical high crest.*

*We also know what the earliest houses in Rome looked like, because small models of them (left) were made to hold the ashes of the dead.*

## Arts and crafts

The Etruscans had a strong influence on Roman civilization. Although we do not understand the Etruscan language yet, we do know that many Roman customs, and even Roman gods, were borrowed from them. The Etruscans were also one channel through which influences from Greece and the East arrived in Italy. Etruscan craftsmanship was exceptional, especially in metalwork (Etruria was well known for its rich mineral resources), and included intricate and costly jewellery.

*This clay figure wearing a tartan robe (left) came from a grave in the Etruscan city of Caere (now Cerveteri). It dates from the late 7th century BC. No one knows the meaning of the movement he is making with his hands.*

## The founder of Rome

According to Roman myth, Rome was founded by Romulus, son of the god of war, Mars. As babies, Romulus and his twin brother Remus were left to die. They were rescued by a she-wolf, and brought up by shepherds. When they had grown up, they founded the city. But they quarrelled over who should rule it, and Romulus killed Remus. This bronze she-wolf (right) is Etruscan and was made about 500 BC. The twins were added about 2,000 years later.

# The City of Rome

Rome, 'the Eternal City', has been at the heart of European history for over 2,000 years. Once a group of small villages clustered on seven hills, it became a republic in 509 BC. As its territory expanded the city thrived and grew but, after the long civil wars of the 1st century BC, the elected officials of the republic were replaced by emperors. Under Augustus, the first emperor, and his successors, Rome became both the largest and the grandest city that Europe had ever seen. Many cities and towns across the Empire became smaller models of Rome and Roman civilization.

*The emperor Augustus (above), whose long reign (27 BC–AD 14) established imperial rule. He holds a standard bearing the imperial eagle.*

## The Roman Forum

The Forum was the chief public square in Rome. In early times it was the centre of religion, trade (there were shops all around), business, political affairs, and even gladiator fights. Gradually, it became more grand. The storekeepers moved out and monumental buildings sprang up (below).

## Police and fire services

Augustus established a paramilitary force against riots and disorders, but most policing was done by ordinary people. Neighbours would combine against a trouble-maker. Fire was a constant danger in the crowded city, and Augustus also set up a body of firefighters, but they could not prevent the fire of AD 64 from burning for six days.

*Coins minted in Rome. Left: The Roman eagle, bird of Jupiter. Right: The double-faced Janus, god of gateways, who looks both ways.*

*A coin of the Roman Republic (right) which shows a citizen casting his vote in an election.*

## Republic and Empire

The Roman Republic was not really democratic, because the patricians (nobles) held the real power. The Romans disliked the idea of rule by a king, and Augustus called himself not 'emperor' but 'first citizen'. He also kept the institutions and officials of the Republic, although they no longer held much power.

*Public speaking was an important skill in Rome, and lawyers and politicians were skilled orators.*

## Senate

Patricians (members of noble families) were represented in the Senate, which was the chief power under the Republic. Originally, the Senate had 300 members; later it had 600. The two elected consuls, who headed the government, were also patricians until plebs were admitted as consuls in 366 BC. Under the emperors, the Senate lost much of its power in government, although it did retain some influence.

## The plebeians

The common people, called plebeians, or plebs, in the early Republic, were not all poor. Some were quite wealthy, but not of noble birth. Under the Republic, the plebeians struggled for greater rights against the dominant patricians, or nobles, who were big landowners. They had some success, gaining their own assembly, their own officials, and equal treatment in law.

*This map shows Rome at its greatest extent, about AD 300. The surrounding wall was 32 miles (51.5 km) long, and the River Tiber was crossed by six bridges. The Colosseum appears in the centre and, below it, imperial palaces and the Circus Maximus.*

## Law and justice

The greatest strength of the Roman Empire, after its armies, was its law. Not even the emperor was above the law and the rights of citizens were firmly upheld in the courts. The Christian apostle, Paul, escaped a sentence of flogging because he was a Roman citizen. Then, as today, cases in court were decided by argument between lawyers, and judgments by elected magistrates were based on earlier decisions.

# Shops and Markets

As Rome expanded, so did its shops and markets. Shops lined the main streets, while high-class craftsmen such as goldsmiths could be found in the oldest commercial centre, the Roman Forum. The biggest shopping complex was the huge covered Market of Trajan, built about AD 110. As well as market stalls, it had five storeys of shops. These establishments included the sellers of fruit and flowers, oil and wine, food, herbs and spices. On one floor there were welfare offices where free food was given out to the needy. On the top floor were fish tanks, some supplied with fresh water from an aqueduct and others filled with sea water from the coast.

## A shop

Shops like this (below) could be found on the streets of any Roman town. They were often self-contained rooms in a house, rented from the owners. The staircase in the background leads to the living quarters of the proprietor and his – or sometimes her – family. More successful shopkeepers had their own house elsewhere.

## Producers and buyers

In early times, most of the goods sold in the shops of a Roman town were produced by the same people who sold them. As time went by, and Rome grew into a city of one million people, a wholesale business developed. Middlemen controlled more and more of the trade – they bought up all the produce of the growers or craftspeople and sold it to stores.

## Shopping

Rich people sent their slaves to do the shopping, and in Rome they probably visited the market on most days. Elsewhere, markets operated once a week. Poorer people did their own shopping, and, as most of them had no kitchens, they bought a lot of ready-cooked food. They could not afford expensive food, and bought mainly bread (straight from the oven), a kind of porridge, and filling vegetables such as beans and lentils.

## Meat

Butchers sold a great variety of meats, perhaps more than we can get from our butchers and supermarkets today. Meat included pork, mutton, goat, beef, wild boar, rabbit, geese, and various other birds, as well as dormice that were specially bred to be eaten. The Romans also ate parts of animals that might seem strange to us – sow's udder, for example, was a great delicacy.

## Bakeries

Flour was milled from grain (left) and was rather coarse compared with the flour we have today. As a result, Roman bread was probably chewier than ours and the dough did not rise so well. Bread was usually baked in the baker's shop, and many bakers milled their own flour.

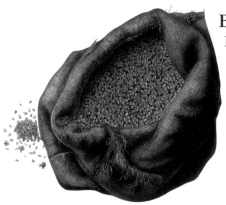

*Above: Bakers took their hot loaves out of the oven with a long-handled spatula, as in this decorative mosaic.*

*The scene on a busy street. It is early in the day and some of the goods are still arriving, but already there are shoppers out on the street. Later in the day, the scene would have been more hectic. The government in Rome often passed regulations to prevent tradesmen taking over the streets.*

*A female innkeeper discusses the bill with a departing traveller.*

## Inside a tavern

Taverns ranged from dark and dirty drinking dens to reasonable restaurants. They usually had a stone counter near the front, with large jars of wine and water (wine was diluted before drinking). In the rear, there were stoves and space to prepare food. Often there was also another more private room at the back, and sometimes a courtyard.

# Inns and Taverns

Rome and the Roman Empire had several kinds of taverns, which provided food and drink, and inns, which also offered a bed for the night. Both also offered entertainment of various kinds, most of it illegal or at least not respectable, such as gambling. Inns and taverns were often situated near the public baths and markets. Few respectable Romans, and certainly no respectable woman, entered a tavern unless they had to. In the eyes of the law, a person who kept a tavern was not much better than a criminal. However, there were some better inns, or hotels, for upper-class travellers such as ambassadors and imperial officials with no other place to stay.

*A sign advertising food and drink, from one of many taverns in the port of Ostia that catered for sailors, traders, and others passing through.*

*This mosaic shows an argument over a game of dice. Gambling peaked in the annual festival of Saturnalia, when all rules were relaxed for a week.*

## Gambling

Taverns in Rome usually had a room at the back for gambling, although there were laws against it. A tavern keeper could not be prosecuted for allowing gambling on his premises, but neither could he sue violent customers who caused damage under the influence of heavy losses or strong wine (or both). Some gamblers cheated, and archaeologists have found loaded dice.

## Eating out

Well-to-do Romans did not go out to eat. Feasts and parties were held at home. In town or in the country, and usually when travelling, they could stay with friends, or friends of friends. Hospitality to strangers was a well-established custom, and for people who had plenty of money and slaves, entertaining visitors was no great chore. If they had nowhere else to stay when travelling far from home, wealthy people stayed at the best inns and often had their food prepared by their own slaves, using the hotel's kitchens.

## Take-aways

Taverns usually had a few simple tables and benches for those who wanted to eat there. Most customers took the food home to eat.

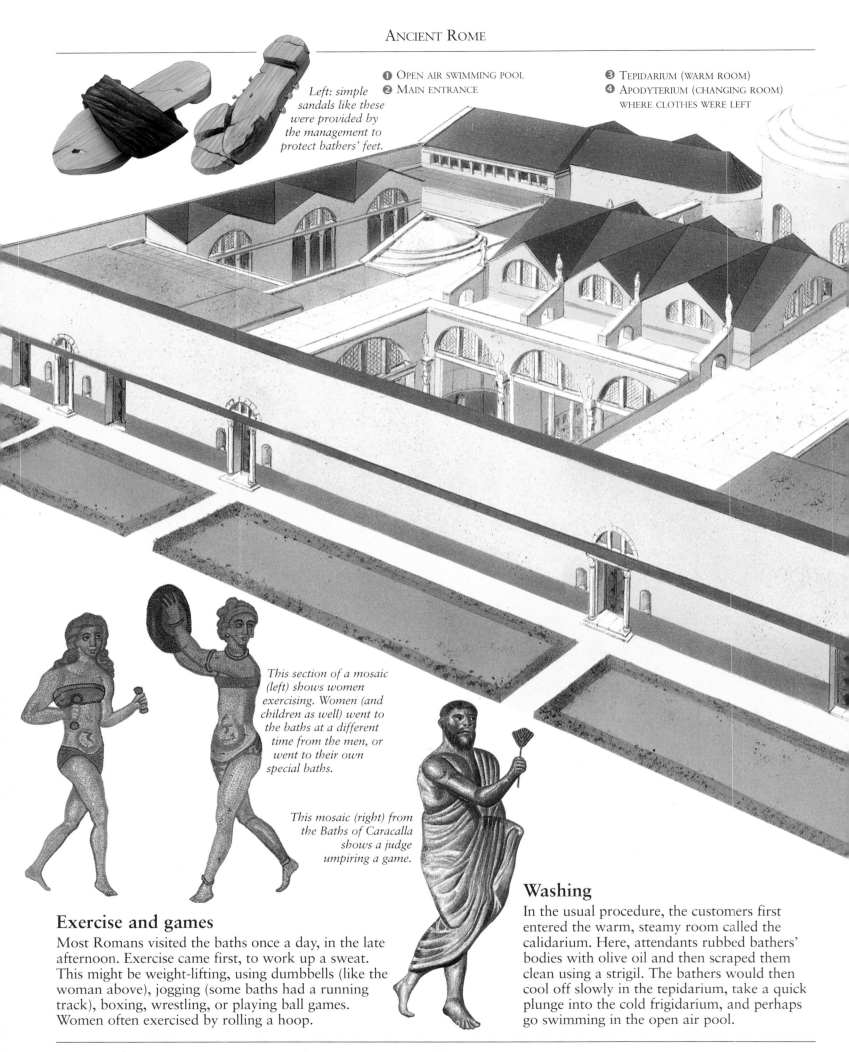

*Left: simple
sandals like these
were provided by
the management to
protect bathers' feet.*

❶ OPEN AIR SWIMMING POOL
❷ MAIN ENTRANCE

❸ TEPIDARIUM (WARM ROOM)
❹ APODYTERIUM (CHANGING ROOM)
WHERE CLOTHES WERE LEFT

*This section of a mosaic
(left) shows women
exercising. Women (and
children as well) went to
the baths at a different
time from the men, or
went to their own
special baths.*

*This mosaic (right) from
the Baths of Caracalla
shows a judge
umpiring a game.*

## Exercise and games

Most Romans visited the baths once a day, in the late
afternoon. Exercise came first, to work up a sweat.
This might be weight-lifting, using dumbbells (like the
woman above), jogging (some baths had a running
track), boxing, wrestling, or playing ball games.
Women often exercised by rolling a hoop.

## Washing

In the usual procedure, the customers first
entered the warm, steamy room called the
calidarium. Here, attendants rubbed bathers'
bodies with olive oil and then scraped them
clean using a strigil. The bathers would then
cool off slowly in the tepidarium, take a quick
plunge into the cold frigidarium, and perhaps
go swimming in the open air pool.

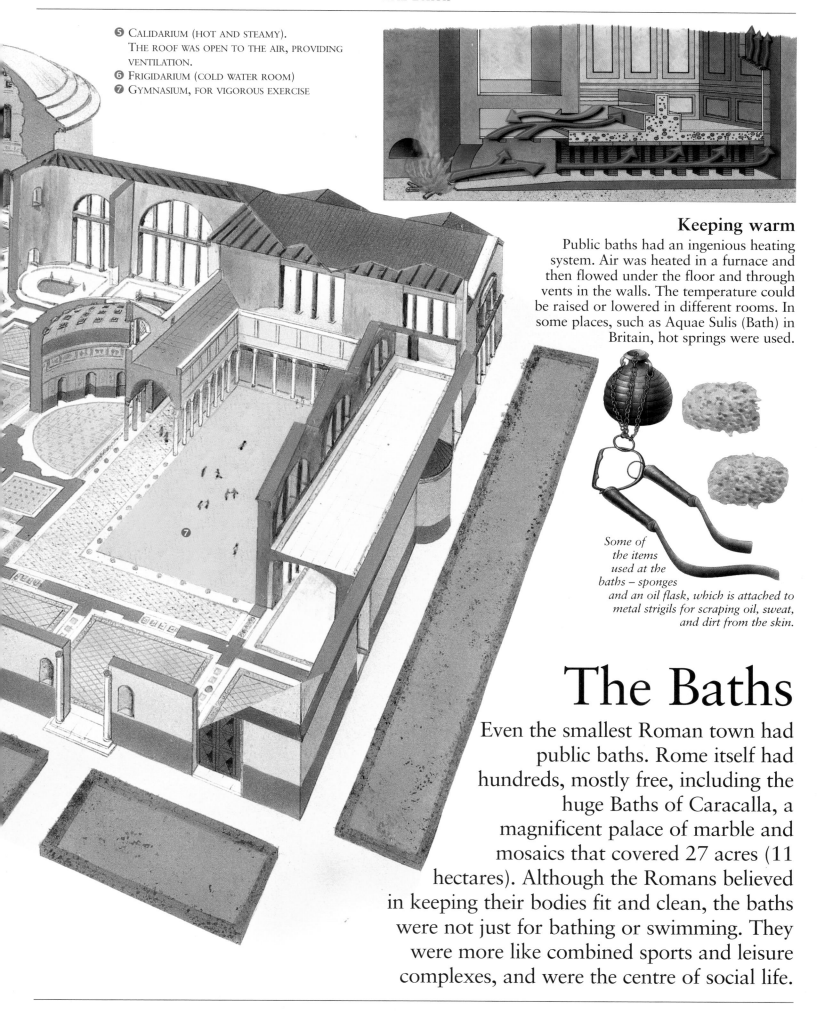

⑤ CALIDARIUM (HOT AND STEAMY).
THE ROOF WAS OPEN TO THE AIR, PROVIDING
VENTILATION.
⑥ FRIGIDARIUM (COLD WATER ROOM)
⑦ GYMNASIUM, FOR VIGOROUS EXERCISE

### Keeping warm

Public baths had an ingenious heating system. Air was heated in a furnace and then flowed under the floor and through vents in the walls. The temperature could be raised or lowered in different rooms. In some places, such as Aquae Sulis (Bath) in Britain, hot springs were used.

*Some of the items used at the baths – sponges and an oil flask, which is attached to metal strigils for scraping oil, sweat, and dirt from the skin.*

# The Baths

Even the smallest Roman town had public baths. Rome itself had hundreds, mostly free, including the huge Baths of Caracalla, a magnificent palace of marble and mosaics that covered 27 acres (11 hectares). Although the Romans believed in keeping their bodies fit and clean, the baths were not just for bathing or swimming. They were more like combined sports and leisure complexes, and were the centre of social life.

# Women

Roman women had more freedom than women in many earlier civilizations. Although Romans believed that a woman's place was in the home, women still took part in social life both with and without their husbands. Well-born women did not need to have jobs or take part in public life. There were female workers, traders, even gladiators, but they were mostly either slaves or freed women (former slaves).

*A woman pours scent into a scent bottle, from a wall painting in a Roman house.*

## Rights of women

Initially women were regarded as the property of their husbands or fathers, but in time upper-class women gained many legal rights. They could manage their own money and business affairs, and their rights to own property were stronger than those of English women 150 years ago. Some lower-class women worked with their husbands, especially in skilled crafts.

## Clothing

Romans wore loose-fitting tunics. A woman's main garment was the ankle-length stola, tied at the waist and below the breasts and worn over a shift or petticoat. Sometimes they wore a cloak (palla) on top. It was a rectangle of cloth, usually draped over one shoulder and around the back, with the other end carried over the arm. It could also be pulled over the head. Most people wore sandals on their feet.

*A necklace of mother-of-pearl and emeralds, a gold snake bracelet, and a ring.*

*Right: Clothes were made of wool, sometimes linen, and silk for the rich.*

## Jewellery

Roman women wore jewellery very similar to the kinds that women wear today – mainly necklaces, bracelets, rings, and earrings (they had pierced ears). For the rich, jewellery was made of gold and gems, and even diamonds from India. Poorer women wore cheaper jewellery made of coloured glass and coloured stones set in bronze.

## Hairstyles

Upper-class women grew their hair long but wore it piled up on the head in different ways. Hairstyles were very elaborate and often took a long time to create and arrange. They sometimes included artificial hair and a wire framework for special effects. Fashionable styles changed as often then as they do now.

*This ivory comb was found in a grave. The letters spell out the words 'Modestina, Vale' ('Farewell, Modestina').*

## Marriage

By the 2nd century AD, relations between husbands and wives were based on affection, not just the wife's obedience. They were partners. Fathers no longer ordered the death of unwanted babies, or chose their daughters' husbands. A Roman wedding included the use of gold rings for the bride and groom and bridesmaids. Another part of a Roman wedding was the sacrifice of a pig or a sheep.

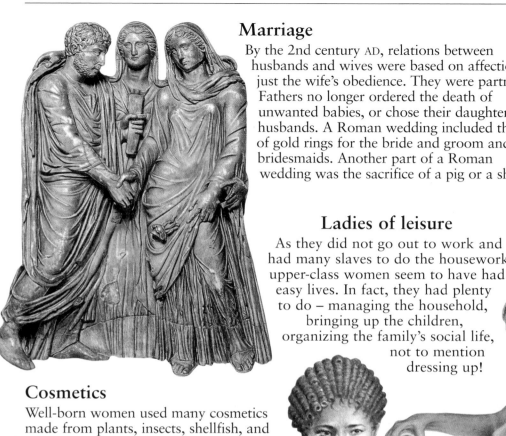

*A nursemaid and a mother give a baby a bath.*

## Ladies of leisure

As they did not go out to work and had many slaves to do the housework, upper-class women seem to have had easy lives. In fact, they had plenty to do – managing the household, bringing up the children, organizing the family's social life, not to mention dressing up!

## Motherhood

A woman's most important job was bringing up children. The emperor made awards to good mothers, who played an important part in young children's education. Boys were often very close to their mothers but more distant from their fathers. We have fewer resources about mothers and daughters (perhaps because all the records we have were written by men).

## Cosmetics

Well-born women used many cosmetics made from plants, insects, shellfish, and other natural materials. These cosmetics were made at home. Some of them were dangerous to health – at one time it was fashionable to use a white face makeup that was made with powdered white lead mixed with oil. This was very bad for the skin. The woman standing at the right in this picture is a trained cosmetician.

## Attendants

There were far more slaves than citizens in the Roman Empire, including household attendants. A lady getting dressed might be attended by four or five female maids. Slaves were property – they could be bought and sold – but household slaves were usually well treated and they could often gain or buy their freedom.

# Children

The Romans treated children as if they were small, but unreliable, adults. Boys were thought old enough to marry at 14, and girls at 12. Children wore the same kind of clothes as adults, and girls in rich families had complicated hairstyles like their mothers. In early times, a Roman father had been like a dictator, and could have his children killed or sold into slavery. But by the 2nd century AD that was illegal (although children from very poor families were probably still sold) and family life was based on affection. The statesman Cicero said that a good father should be respected by his children. Some fathers were criticized for spoiling their children, especially sons, who grew into selfish adults.

*A charm in the form of a gold pendant, called a bulla, was worn by free-born Roman boys and girls to keep evil spirits away. Poorer children wore leather ones.*

## Games and toys

Well-off Romans had plenty of time for sports and play. Popular games included 'Robbers', which was like a simple form of chess, and a board game called 'Twelve Lines', which was like backgammon. Archaeologists have found a huge variety of toys, including marbles, wooden and cloth dolls, carved animals, dolls' houses, rocking-horses, and toys on wheels. Boys liked imitating chariot races with toy chariots.

*A home-made rag doll from Roman Egypt. It survived nearly 2,000 years because it was buried in the dry sand.*

## Education

Well-off boys, and sometimes girls, went to their first school at the age of seven. Their education was mostly learning things off by heart, and teachers often used the cane on their students. Some Romans were not happy with this system and complained about it. A small number of students went on to higher education, mostly studying literature, and boys finished at a school of rhetoric, which taught public-speaking skills. A few from top families might then visit the cities of Greece, which the Romans regarded as the heart of learning.

*Above: A boy's first teacher was his father, although in later times he usually had a tutor, who was often an educated slave.*

## Pets

Most Roman households had guard dogs. Collar tags have been found that give the name and address of the owner. Richer children had many pets. Birds were popular, including songbirds like nightingales.

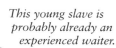

*This young slave is probably already an experienced waiter.*

## Reading and writing

Those who had a full education could read and write in both Latin (the Romans' native language) and Greek. 'Books' were in the form of scrolls, and were very rare because they had to be copied by hand. The form of paper they were written on was also expensive, because it was made either from papyrus reeds imported from Egypt or from animal skins (vellum).

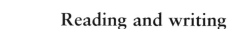

## Slave children

Some owners had the children of their household slaves properly educated, but for most slaves, from an early age, life consisted only of work. They did not necessarily have a family life, because they belonged not only to their parents but also to their owners. Still, there is a character in many Roman stories called the 'crafty slave' – he was cleverer than his owners, whether or not he was educated.

*Ink was made from soot, pens from reed or metal. The instrument on the right of the pen is a bronze stylus, used for writing on reusable wax tablets at school or home.*

# Building and Technology

The Romans did not produce such great thinkers and artists as their forerunners, the ancient Greeks. But in practical affairs – such as building and engineering – they were far superior. When it came to building roads, bridges, or sewers, or making machines and tools, no other people in Europe reached the standards set by the Romans until well over a thousand years after the Roman Empire had disappeared.

*A crane being used on a monumental building, 1st century AD.*

## Engineering

Although Romans lacked artificial engines to provide power, they had animals (oxen and horses) and a huge supply of manpower (slaves). Tread-wheels, bigger versions of the wheels that modern pet hamsters like to play in, provided the power to pump water from deep mines or to operate lifting devices (like the one above).

*The design of the Pantheon, to which the emperor Hadrian himself probably contributed, shows a skilful sense of space. The diameter of the dome is exactly the same as the distance between the top of the dome and the floor – a huge ball would fit exactly inside. This vast circular space is lit by a single great round opening at the top of the dome.*

## The Pantheon

The Pantheon ('temple to all the gods') is the finest surviving building from ancient Rome. It was built by the cultured emperor Hadrian in 118–125. The dome is an amazing 142 feet (43.3 m) in diameter, and its construction was made possible by the Roman invention of concrete. It remained the largest dome in the world until the 20th century.

*Roman roads were so well made that some still exist. The Appian Way (left) was the main road leading south from Rome.*

*Underneath the city streets lead pipes carried fresh water and, at a deeper level, sewers carried away waste from lavatories. Houses not connected to the sewer system had cesspits.*

## Plumbing

Roman water supply and drains were superior to anything in Europe until the 19th century. In the city, fresh water was carried in lead or pottery pipes to public wells, fountains, and baths, and also to the houses of wealthy residents. As far as possible, water was moved by gravity; for example, a raised tank would operate a fountain. Pipes were fitted with valves to prevent water running the wrong way.

## Roads

The famous Roman roads were built by the army, as straight as possible, for troops to move around the empire quickly. They were equally useful to traders and other travellers. Materials varied, but there was usually a deep foundation of small stones with heavy slabs on top. They were lined by kerbstones, and the surface sloped down from the centre so the rain ran off.

## Water power

When the wheat harvest was gathered, the grains of corn were taken to a mill, like this one in southern France. Water from a river or stream was channelled through to the mill, where it flowed over a water wheel. As the force of the falling water turned the wheel, it made power to turn grindstones. Grain was crushed between the stones, and this was how flour was made.

## Bridges

Unlike the Greeks, whose architecture was all straight lines (the 'post and beam' method), the Romans developed the arch (and the dome). The arch allowed the Romans to span wide spaces with their bridges and aqueducts, many of which are still standing today. Aqueducts carried fresh water to towns from springs high in the hills, sometimes many miles away.

*The Milvian Bridge north of Rome was built about 100 BC. It carried the Via Flaminia, the main road to Etruria.*

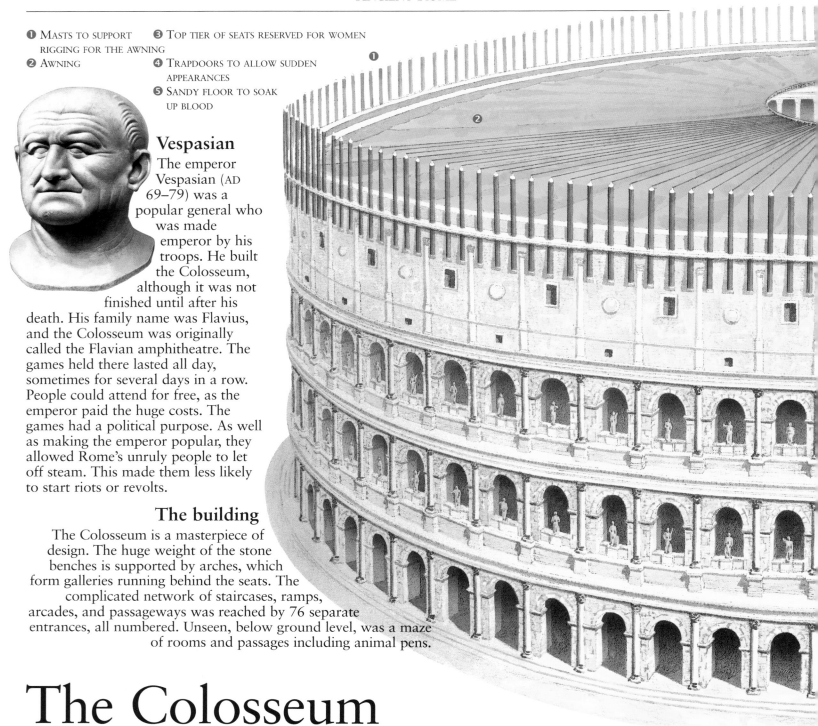

❶ MASTS TO SUPPORT RIGGING FOR THE AWNING

❷ AWNING

❸ TOP TIER OF SEATS RESERVED FOR WOMEN

❹ TRAPDOORS TO ALLOW SUDDEN APPEARANCES

❺ SANDY FLOOR TO SOAK UP BLOOD

## Vespasian

The emperor Vespasian (AD 69–79) was a popular general who was made emperor by his troops. He built the Colosseum, although it was not finished until after his death. His family name was Flavius, and the Colosseum was originally called the Flavian amphitheatre. The games held there lasted all day, sometimes for several days in a row. People could attend for free, as the emperor paid the huge costs. The games had a political purpose. As well as making the emperor popular, they allowed Rome's unruly people to let off steam. This made them less likely to start riots or revolts.

### The building

The Colosseum is a masterpiece of design. The huge weight of the stone benches is supported by arches, which form galleries running behind the seats. The complicated network of staircases, ramps, arcades, and passageways was reached by 76 separate entrances, all numbered. Unseen, below ground level, was a maze of rooms and passages including animal pens.

# The Colosseum

Every Roman town had an amphitheatre, a large arena where popular entertainments were staged. The largest was the Colosseum in Rome, which was built between about AD 70 and 80. An oval arena surrounded by seating, it measured 617 by 512 feet (188 by 156 m), and was 157 feet (48 m) high. It held about 50,000 spectators. The seats could be covered by a gigantic awning for protection against the sun. Roughly half the building still stands in the middle of modern Rome, and it is the most impressive building in the city.

*A coin of the emperor Titus (AD 79–81), showing the Colosseum as it was when first built. The top storey, above the three rows of arches, is hung with shields.*

*Right: With shin guards but no protection for chests, gladiators' armour was flashy rather than actually useful.*

*There were many kinds of gladiators. This is the helmet of a so-called 'heavily armed' gladiator (hoplomachus), but his upper body might be unprotected like the clay figures above.*

## Gladiators

Most gladiators were slaves, including prisoners of war, and criminals. They were trained at gladiator schools, but their lives were short as they sometimes fought to the death. However, a successful gladiator could win his freedom, and big prize money as well. Some became popular heroes, and a few gladiators were volunteers. Fighting skill and putting on a good show for the audience were more important than killing an opponent quickly.

*The games were so popular that they were often the subject of decoration in Roman houses. The mosaic below shows different types of gladiators, including a 'net man' (retiarius) whose weapons were a net (to entangle his opponent) and a trident (top right).*

*Animal fights were popular. This 'bestiarius', an animal fighter, is armed and stands a chance against the leopard. Condemned criminals had their hands tied, and were simply torn to pieces.*

## Blood and death

The Romans called their entertainments 'games' but they consisted mainly of fights between gladiators and public executions of criminals. Blood and cruelty – the torture of humans and animals – was what the Roman crowd liked to see. This may seem disgusting (as some Romans thought it was) but some people today also enjoy watching extreme violence and cruelty, though on TV and film.

# Circus and Theatre

The Romans' favourite sport was chariot-racing. The main race track or stadium, called the Circus Maximus, was one of the oldest buildings in Rome. It was close to the emperor's palace. An underground tunnel led from the palace to his private box.

## Chariot-racing

Racing was a highly professional sport. Riders belonged to different teams, with their own colours, patrons, fans, and staff of trainers, vets, blacksmiths, and carpenters. The charioteers were often slaves at first, and could buy their freedom with their prize money. One champion, named Scorpus, won 2,000 races and was a rich man when he died in a crash aged 27.

## The theatre

Early Roman theatres were temporary wooden buildings. Stone theatres (right) were built after 55 BC. They had permanent architectural sets, a raised stage, and tiers of seats in a half circle. Audiences liked comedies best, and these were mostly based on Greek plays.

## Actors and masks

Actors had a low status in society. Most were slaves, or former slaves. They wore masks with exaggerated expressions (left) to represent the type of character that they were playing. The same actor could play several different parts by wearing different masks.

## Roman drama

There were few Roman playwrights to compare with the Greeks. The best of the few whose work has survived was Seneca, and he wrote his plays to be read rather than performed. By AD 200 drama had almost disappeared and was replaced by crude variety performances and wild animal shows.

*Chariots were very light and were drawn by four horses. They raced around the Circus Maximus seven times, and the sharp turns at each end caused frequent accidents.*

# Soldiers

The basis of the Roman Empire was the Roman army, the first truly professional army of volunteer citizens in history. The legionaries (a legion contained up to 5,000 men) signed on for 20 years. Apart from fighting, the main job of the legionaries was guarding the frontiers of the Empire, and many of them never saw Italy. As a result they came to feel greater loyalty to their own generals than to the distant emperor. This became a problem when rival generals, supported by their own men, fought for the imperial throne.

## Armour

In the 1st–2nd centuries AD, Roman soldiers wore a metal helmet, with neck guard, and armour breastplate, and they carried a shield that protected them from neck to knee. Jointed plates, mounted on leather strips, allowed free movement of the shoulders. Chain mail, made of metal links, was worn earlier. Auxiliary troops (allies of the Romans or men who fought for pay) wore their own kind of armour.

*The emperor Hadrian (117–138) decided the Empire was big enough and set about creating frontiers that could be defended easily. One result was Hadrian's Wall in northern Britain, which ran across the country south of modern Scotland. It had a fort every mile, with two watchtowers between each fort. Larger forts, like the one shown here (left), provided back-up.*

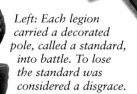

*Left: Each legion carried a decorated pole, called a standard, into battle. To lose the standard was considered a disgrace.*

*A Roman foot soldier's chief weapon in hand-to-hand fighting was the short sword. He also carried a spear. The steel blade of this sword has rusted, but the gold and silver hilt has survived undamaged.*

## Forts

Wherever a legion was stationed, it built its own fort following the standard plan. It was surrounded by a stone-and-earth wall with towers at each corner and two more guarding the four gates. The main buildings were barracks for the troops, houses for the officers, and a large house at the centre for the general. Also included were offices, stables, stores, workshops, baths, hospitals, and a prison.

*The Romans invented a variety of machines for attacking enemy towns. This siege tower (left), with soldiers inside, could be pushed up to the walls where the soldiers jumped out to attack the defenders.*

## The Praetorian Guard

These were elite troops, originally the emperor's bodyguard, who were paid three times as much as ordinary legionaries. They were stationed on the outskirts of Rome, so they could act fast in the case of a serious riot. They came to have a dangerous influence on politics in the late 2nd century AD. In fact, in AD 193 they killed the emperor and offered the job to whoever would pay them the most.

*An attack on a town. In a siege, it was often unnecessary to do any fighting. The attackers would build their own fortifications around the town and wait for hunger or disease to force the defenders to surrender.*

*Elephants frightened an enemy who had never seen them before, but they were not useful against experienced soldiers. A few well-aimed arrows or spears made them panic, often causing more trouble for their own side than for the enemy.*

## The Punic Wars

By 264 BC, the little Roman republic had conquered its neighbours in mainland Italy and started to fight in places like Sicily as well. But Sicily was claimed by Carthage, in North Africa. Rome's three wars against Carthage are known as the Punic Wars and went on for more than a century, from 264 to 146 BC. They ended with the complete destruction of Carthage.

*Hannibal crossed the Alps with elephants, although only one survived to carry him through Italy. The Romans also used elephants during the conquest of Britain in AD 43.*

## Hannibal

During the Second Punic War (218–201 BC) the great Carthaginian general Hannibal invaded Italy from Spain. He crossed the Alps in winter and took the Romans by surprise. He remained in Italy for 13 years. The Romans could not defeat him, but Hannibal was unable to capture Rome. In the end the Romans sent an army to North Africa. Hannibal had to return to defend Carthage, and he was defeated.

## Vestal Virgins

Vesta, a sister of Juno, was associated with the prosperity of the Roman state. Her circular shrine (below) was in the Roman Forum, and she was served by the Vestal Virgins, who were Rome's most important priestesses. Daughters of noble families, they were chosen as young girls and each served for 30 years, keeping Vesta's permanent flame alight.

### Sacrifices and offerings

Roman religion included complicated ceremonies in which offerings such as wine and incense were made and an animal was sacrificed. The animal was first sprinkled with salted cakes prepared by the Vestal Virgins. Afterwards, its insides were examined by special priests who could foretell the intentions of the gods by 'reading' the liver.

# Religion

The chief Roman god was Jupiter, who headed a family of gods and goddesses. Eventually they became identified with the gods of ancient Greece – Jupiter with the Greek Zeus, his wife Juno with her Greek equivalent, Hera, and so on. Worship and sacrifices were carried out to please the gods. As time went by, Romans adopted a number of foreign gods and cults. Roman religion was closely linked with politics. Although Julius Caesar was an atheist, he held the role of chief priest.

### The imperial cult

Augustus, the first Roman emperor, understood the political importance of religion. He encouraged the idea that the emperor himself was divine or semi-divine. Dissatisfied subjects were less likely to rebel against a god! Emperor-worship never became a true religion, but was a strong cult in some parts. The emperor Commodus (above) insisted that the Senate call him a god and identified himself with the mythical hero Hercules, who wore a lion-skin cloak.

## Household gods

Household gods, penates, and manes (spirits of dead ancestors) were worshipped in the home. Most families had a little shrine in the atrium. There were other minor gods or spirits, such as the lares (right) who inhabited a particular place. Their shrines could often be seen at crossroads.

*Above: This wall painting shows Bacchus, god of wine, dressed in a cloak of grapes with his attendant panther. He was identified with the formidable Greek god Dionysus, whose worship included extravagant mystical rites.*

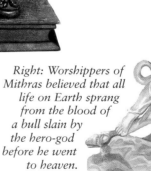

*Right: This decorative bronze statue shows Fortuna, the Roman goddess of luck or good fortune. She was the focus of several cults in later times. Among other things, she was believed to help women who wanted to have children.*

## Mithraism

Mithraism, a religion from Iran, became popular among soldiers. Mithras was part sun-god and part hero. He was worshipped in dim cells or caves that were most unlike the great temples of the Roman gods. Mithraism did not admit women.

*Right: Worshippers of Mithras believed that all life on Earth sprang from the blood of a bull slain by the hero-god before he went to heaven.*

## Christianity

Christianity was founded at roughly the same time as the Roman Empire. Christians, however, refused to worship the Roman gods, which was treason. Most emperors ignored Christians as far as possible, but sometimes they were hunted down and killed, especially in the 3rd century. Yet Christianity gained more and more believers. In 313 the religion was granted official toleration by the emperor Constantine (306–337). He made Christianity the state religion.

## Mystery cults

The liveliest religions in the Roman Empire were the foreign 'mystery cults'. Roman rulers were suspicious of them. They feared that they might be a cover for treason, but usually tolerated them. The worship of Cybele the 'Great Mother' originated in Anatolia (Turkey) and was popular with women. Her worship included music and dancing, and this carving (above) of one of her priests shows instruments used to worship her.

*The sistrum (below), a kind of musical rattle, was used by the priests of the Egyptian goddess Isis – hers was one of the most popular mystery cults in Rome. The sistrum's sound was believed to drive away evil spirits.*

*After 313, when the edict of Milan granted tolerance to Christianity, Christians were free to build their own churches (right). They copied the type of Roman building called a basilica, which was a long hall divided by rows of columns.*

# A Roman House

Wealthy Romans were very rich indeed. They often owned a country estate as well as a town house. Although they lacked modern services such as electricity, living conditions were very comfortable thanks to their many servants (actually slaves). Houses followed a traditional pattern, although this varied in different parts of the Empire. From the outside, only a few tiny windows high up on the walls were visible. The main rooms were grouped around the atrium, an open area in the centre. Country houses, or villas, were usually attached to a large estate or farm. Town houses were grouped in the fashionable parts of a town. In Rome itself, only the very rich could afford to own them.

*A small stove made of pottery. A charcoal fire heated food in pots which rested on the top. Some kitchens had larger stoves, with a flat top where pots could be boiled or meat grilled.*

## The private house

Houses of stone or brick, sometimes plastered, were usually built on one floor. Especially in Rome, where space was limited, part might have an upper floor. Some had a basement, a maze of small rooms where the slaves lived.

## Decoration

Although rooms were sparsely furnished, they were richly decorated with paintings, carvings, and mosaics. Often, all the walls were covered with paintings of abstract patterns or realistic pictures, or panels of different colours, while the floor was covered in mosaics. Mosaics are pictures made by arranging small cubes of different-coloured stone or glass. Mosaics were often designed in geometric black and white patterns.

❶ *ROOFS WERE GENERALLY COVERED WITH FLAT AND CURVED TILES.*

❷ *SOMETIMES ROOMS WERE RENTED OUT AND ROOMS ON THE STREET WERE OFTEN TURNED INTO SHOPS. CUSTOMERS DID NOT HAVE TO ENTER THE SHOP, BECAUSE THE COUNTER WAS RIGHT AT THE FRONT.*

❸ *BEDROOMS WERE USUALLY SMALL, AND FEW MEMBERS OF THE HOUSEHOLD HAD ONE OF THEIR OWN.*

❹ MAIN ENTRANCE

❺ VESTIBULE, OR HALL

❻ SHOP

*Mosaic-makers became so skilful that it was hard to tell their pictures from paintings. This mosaic of doves comes from the emperor Hadrian's villa at Tivoli, near Rome. The villa was a country estate the size of a small town.*

## Furniture

Rich Romans often owned valuable and varied furniture, but to our eyes today their homes would look underfurnished. Large pieces, such as hefty wardrobes, were especially rare. Wealthy families often moved between town and country houses, and they liked furniture that could be moved from house to house or room to room. Although they had chairs and stools, the Romans preferred reclining on couches at mealtimes.

*This double-ended bed (above) does not look comfortable, but it would have had a mattress, blankets, and pillows on top. Like the folding stool (below) it is made mainly of bronze. Furniture was a type of property and was regarded as an investment, so the wealthy often had furniture made of costly materials.*

⑧ ROMANS LOVED THEIR GARDENS, WHICH HAD STATUES AND PERHAPS A POOL OR FOUNTAIN. ROOMS NEXT TO THE GARDEN, USUALLY INCLUDING THE DINING ROOM, ENJOYED NATURAL LIGHT AND A BEAUTIFUL VIEW.

*Glass-making was one of the finest crafts, and the houses of rich people might contain glass vessels (above) made in places as far away as Syria and western Germany. Silver jugs, bowls, and wine cups were also made in different countries. They displayed wealth, and, in times of need, they could be melted down for money.*

⑨ THE PERISTYLE WAS A ROOFED COLONNADE AROUND A GARDEN.

⑩ THE DINING ROOM OR TRICLINIUM HAD COUCHES AROUND THREE WALLS. PEOPLE ATE OFF SMALL PORTABLE TABLES. IF THERE WERE MANY GUESTS, THEY MOVED INTO THE PERISTYLE OR ATRIUM.

*Right: A sculpture of a child playing with a mask. Sculptures, made of bronze or marble, were often placed in gardens and open spaces as well as inside houses.*

⑪ THE ATRIUM WAS THE CENTRE OF THE MAIN PART OF THE VILLA WHERE THE HOUSEHOLD GODS WERE KEPT. RAINWATER FELL THROUGH THE OPEN SKYLIGHT INTO A POOL IN THE FLOOR AND DRAINED INTO A TANK.

⑫ THE KITCHEN WAS QUITE SMALL. IT HAD A COOKER AND A SINK. THE LAVATORY WAS NEARBY, SO THAT IT COULD BE FLUSHED WITH THE USED WASHING-UP WATER.

## Running the household

A wealthy household, which usually included relatives such as elderly grandparents, or sometimes visitors, required a full-time manager. This was the job of the owner's wife. She gave the slaves their daily orders, looked after young children, and made sure that the household ran smoothly.

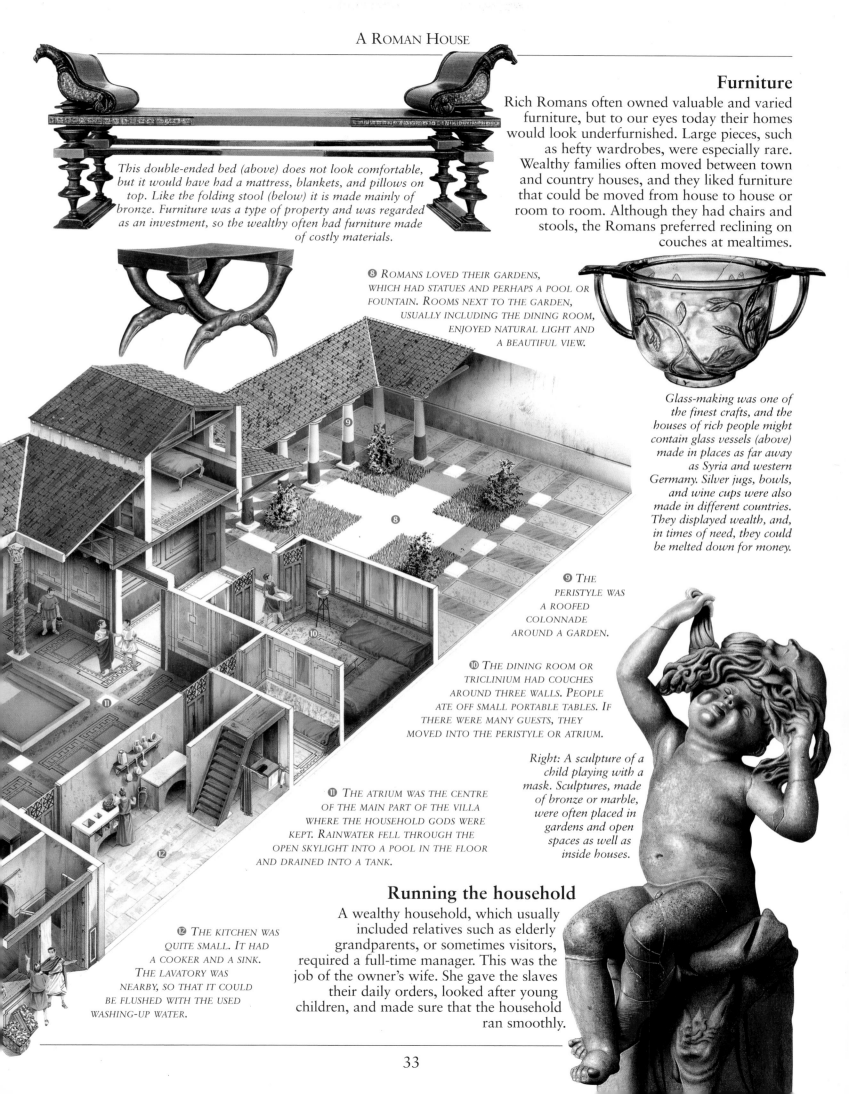

# Farming

The best and most useful way for a gentleman to make his living, said Cicero (106–43 BC), was as a farmer. He should have said landowner, because the sort of farmer he meant had labourers and slaves to do the work. Farming was the most important occupation in the Roman Empire and, as the basis of the Empire's wealth, farming was even more important than trade. We think of Romans as city people, but far more 'citizens' lived in the country than in the towns. Farm sizes varied greatly. Early on, most were fairly small and run by families, but increasingly these were bought to form part of much larger estates.

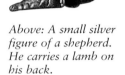

*Above: A small silver figure of a shepherd. He carries a lamb on his back.*

*Above: Picking apples. Besides apples and grapes, figs, pears, and pomegranates were common fruits. Later came peaches, apricots, and a few lemons – but no oranges.*

## Harvesting olives

Olives were one of the most important crops, especially for their oil, although they were also eaten as food. Olives will grow in soil too poor for cereals, and from the 2nd century AD, when Italy could no longer produce enough, thousands of miles of olive groves were planted in Spain and North Africa. Olives were harvested by hitting the trees' branches to knock the olives to the ground, and then they were loaded into baskets and carried to the olive press.

*Right: Wagons like these would have been seen over much of the Roman Empire.*

## Farm transport

Although the Romans had horses, mules, and donkeys, for heavy loads they used oxen as draught animals. Farmers' carts and wagons were no different from those still used in parts of Europe today. Some may have been based on Celtic designs.

## Honey

Sugar was unknown in Roman Europe, and honey was the chief sweetener. Like wine-making, the secrets of bee-keeping were understood long before the Roman Empire. Hives were made of pottery or sometimes wood, and were arranged in rows. Different types of honey were produced and different techniques used in different places. Thyme-based honey from Attica (Greece) had a high reputation in Rome.

*This plough (below) was simply a spike that broke up the ground for sowing. Later, the Romans adopted a Celtic type of plough, which was better as it also turned the soil.*

## Animals

Sheep were kept mainly for their wool, but also for milk. The Romans made cheese from both sheep's and goats' milk. Some big farms experimented with selective breeding. Like sheep, pigs were easy to keep as they could partly fend for themselves – but they did need to be guarded from thieves and predators. Beef was less popular than pork, and people preferred sheep's milk to that of cows. Cattle were raised as working animals and for leather, and donkeys did lighter farmwork. Chickens provided eggs and meat.

*Above: Pork was the Romans' favourite meat, and pigs were kept all over the Empire. They were easy to feed in the winter and in the summer they foraged in the woods.*

## Cereals

Rome's huge growth as a city meant that it soon depended on imports for its main food supplies. By about AD 100 the fertile North African provinces were 'Rome's breadbasket'. These provinces produced about 750,000 tons of wheat every year. Other cereals included barley (used for brewing beer), oats, and rye. The Romans did not use rice.

*Below: Trampling grapes into juice to make wine. The heavy sticks assist the crushing, and, like the linked hands, help to prevent the men slipping.*

## Wine

Wine-making was an ancient art, and vineyards existed all over the Empire, even in Britain. Wine was the favourite Roman drink. After AD 100 Rome's wine mainly came from abroad. However, vines flourished in Italy. The finest vintage wine was grown on the slopes of Mount Vesuvius, and in earlier times Italian growers had exported wine to northern Europe. Grapes were also grown for eating and for grape juice.

# A Roman Kitchen

The Romans had fewer foods than we do (no potatoes or tomatoes), but they ate a great variety all the same (even some foods that we don't eat, such as grilled dormouse!). Their food may have been healthier than ours, without any chemicals and additives. If they could afford to, the Romans ate well. On country estates nearly all the food was home-produced, but in the crowded city of Rome food supply was big business. The emperors made sure that the poorer classes were supplied with free bread. Otherwise, food was brought in by the many tradesmen. These included specialists like the *peponarii*, who sold melons. Commerce was complex, but less so than today. The grocer often grew the vegetables that he sold, and the fishmonger sometimes caught his own fish.

SMALL PAN

COLANDER

*This pan and colander are just like those we use today, except that they are bronze, not steel.*

WATER HEATER

## Cooking

Many houses did not have kitchens, so Romans ate a lot of take-aways. In big houses and country villas slaves did all the cooking and served the meals. There were many slaves working in such a kitchen, under a head chef, probably with a wine steward and other specialists.

*Fresh fruit and vegetables were stored in baskets. Other food, including wine and olive oil, was stored in clay pots or jars (amphorae).*

## Preparing a dinner party

Dinner parties for the rich, which began in the early afternoon, might last many hours. These were often held outside. The upper-class custom of reclining to eat made it difficult to squeeze many guests into a dining room, unless they were somewhere like the emperor's palace. A small army of slaves prepared and served a variety of dishes, often starting with eggs and ending with fruit. Dishes such as meat and vegetables were served separately.

## Utensils

Knives of various kinds were used in the kitchen, and table knives were used at meals for cutting meat. Wooden ladles and metal spoons were also used to serve, but the Romans preferred to eat with their fingers. They did not use forks much.

GRATER

FENNEL SEEDS

ROSEMARY

STONE MORTAR AND PESTLE

ANISE

BASIL

CUMIN

PARSLEY

*Fine glassware, like these flasks, was more fragile and costly than pottery. It was probably used for serving rather than storage.*

## Food

The Romans grew many vegetables, such as asparagus, cabbage, carrots, cucumber, leeks, lettuce, onions, squash, peas, and beans. They probably used up to 100 different herbs and spices, some grown in gardens and some gathered wild. They ate many different kinds of meat, fish, and game.

## Baking

In the city most people bought bread from a bakery, but houses with kitchens often had an oven. Long-handled trays, like this one on the left, might have been used for baking smaller items inside very hot ovens.

CASSEROLE

*Food was cooked using charcoal or wood that burned on a solid platform, like a barbecue.*

WATER STOVE

## Fresh food

For Roman cooks, like all others before refrigerators were invented, keeping food fresh was a problem. Some houses may have had larders or pantries, others had cool cellars. The Mediterranean provided a rich variety of fish, but the difficulty of getting it fresh to a kitchen in Rome made it expensive. One reason for the popularity of the strong fish sauce called garum may have been that it disguised the flavour of food that was past its use-by date.

JARS FOR OLIVE OIL AND WINE

GRILL WITH PLACES FOR POTS ON THE BACK

# Workers and Crafts

*Below: decorative mosaic. The tesserae could be as small as 0.04 inches (1mm) square, so that the mosaic looked like a painting.*

People in Rome were always complaining about the noise. The trouble was that Rome was a huge manufacturing city. The commotion came from hundreds of different crafts – from the clang of blacksmiths' hammers and the roar of glassblowers' furnaces, to the shouts of the wagoners and the rattle and thud of carts on cobbled streets.

Thousands of workshops were scattered throughout the city, not confined to an industrial area like they often are today. There were other differences too – producers were also sales people. The man who sold you a knife was the same man who made it. Butchers and grocers were also farmers. Women could be found in many trades, but generally they were far outnumbered by the men.

## Cloth

After food production, clothes and fabrics made up one of the biggest industries (including crafts such as spinning, weaving and dyeing). Clothes were generally simple but Romans liked bright colours and weavers made exotic decorative fabrics. The army was a major customer of the clothing industry.

## Mosaics

Romans decorated their houses with wall paintings and mosaics. Mosaics are pictures or patterns made out of small pebbles, or cubes of differently coloured stone or glass (tesserae) fitted together in a bed of mortar. Stone mosaics in colour or in black and white often covered floors. They were so popular that they were mass-produced; people could buy a ready-made mosaic panel or 'emblema' to set in the floor.

*Roman jewellers were experts at making cameos, small relief carvings in hard stone. Portraits were a popular subject.*

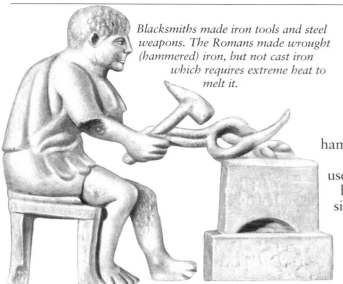

Blacksmiths made iron tools and steel weapons. The Romans made wrought (hammered) iron, but not cast iron which requires extreme heat to melt it.

## Silver

Conquests of silver-mining regions in Spain and Turkey brought large quantities of silver to Rome. A lot of this silver was made into coins. The rest was worked by silversmiths who hammered it into plates and decorated it with techniques similar to those used today. Wealthy people sometimes had small silver statues and domestic silverware, especially cups, gilded with gold leaf.

*The silver cup, decorated with skeletons, warns that life is short. It belonged to a silver service containing 109 pieces.*

## Pottery

Pottery was made on a wheel or in a mould and fired in a special kiln. Most potters specialized in a certain type. On the tables of the wealthy the dinner service might be high-quality shiny red Samian ware, which would reflect the light from elaborately moulded and coloured oil lamps. Plain earthenware bowls and dishes were much more common. Pottery was also used by builders, especially for roof tiles.

*Household items such as cups, bowls, and mirrors came in many forms and were made from a range of materials.*

## Glass

Glass vessels were rare until glass-blowing was invented in the 1st century BC. Before long, glassworks existed all over the empire. It was even made in sheets for windows. Glass vessels could be decorated in several different ways, including using the cameo process. Some glassworkers were highly skilled and, as we know from their surviving work, their glass was as beautiful as any made since.

*In this scene a slave is buying a new kitchen knife. Cooks' knives often had decorative handles of carved bone or ivory.*

# Apartment Blocks

The great mass of people in the cities lived in apartment blocks that could be up to six storeys high. Some were attractive, but most were built with cheap materials and had weak foundations. As many Romans complained, hardly a day passed without one collapsing somewhere. Cicero owned a block and said of it, 'Even the mice have moved out.' Fires were common, and caused many deaths when people were caught on upper floors. There were no toilets, except on the ground floor. Water had to be carried up the stairs using buckets.

*Fine glassware (above) could be found in the homes of the rich.*

### Higher living

By the 2nd century AD some apartments were built for rich tenants. They were built of brick, and plastered. The better apartments roughly followed the usual plan for a Roman house, and on the ground floor even had gardens. Unlike others, they had their own lavatory and kitchen. Their occupants could afford expensive furnishings.

❶ SHOPS OCCUPIED MANY STREET-LEVEL UNITS, AND SOME HAD MEZZANINES OR UPPER FLOORS.

❷ WALLS WERE GENERALLY THIN, AND UNTIL THE 1ST CENTURY BC THEY WERE OFTEN MADE OF RUBBLE.

❸ SOME APARTMENTS HAD A BALCONY.

## Owners and tenants

Apartment blocks were usually built as an investment. The builder might let the whole block to a tenant, who in turn rented out apartments to individual families. The owner could make more money if he just kept patching up a shaky block rather than rebuilding it. A fire would attract a rich speculator, hoping to buy the site cheap from the distressed owner. Then he would rebuild it and make a large profit from the rent.

## Windows

Glass windows were rare for apartment blocks. Some windows were covered by grilles, others had wooden shutters. There was nothing to keep out the cold without blocking the light. Apart from unglazed windows, these blocks looked much like similar buildings in Italian towns today.

*Right: An iron grille covering a window.*

## Heat and light

Apartment blocks tended to be cold in winter and hot in summer, especially on the upper floors. There was no central heating, except occasionally on the ground floor, although many people had small portable stoves. Artificial light came only from candles and oil lamps, which were obvious fire hazards.

*An earthenware oil lamp. With such poor means of lighting, Romans got up at dawn to make the most of daylight.*

④ WINDOWS WERE OFTEN LARGER THAN IN PRIVATE HOUSES, TO LET IN MORE LIGHT.

# The Port of Ostia

Ostia was a town on the coast at the mouth of the River Tiber, 15.5 miles (25 km) downstream from Rome. During the early Republic it was a naval base, but it soon developed into a big commercial port and was later called Portus Romae, meaning 'the port of Rome'. By the time of the emperor Claudius (41–54) the river mouth was silting up, so a new harbour was built 1.8 miles (3 km) to the north. A huge ship, which had brought a stone obelisk from Egypt, was sunk in the harbour as a platform for a lighthouse. A small town developed there too, but Ostia remained the main centre for business.

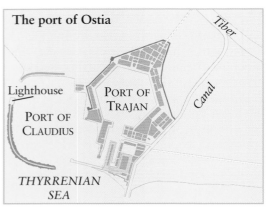

*Above: The harbour of Claudius is shown to the left. It was far from perfect, and a storm in AD 62 destroyed 200 grain ships moored inside. The emperor Trajan (98–117) built a better-protected six-sided harbour big enough for 300 ships. Canals connected it with the Tiber.*

*Big sea-going ships could not sail up the Tiber, and their cargo was transferred to river boats at Ostia. In this fragment of sculpture (left) a river boat is towed out to a merchant ship and, on the right, merchant and captain celebrate a successful voyage.*

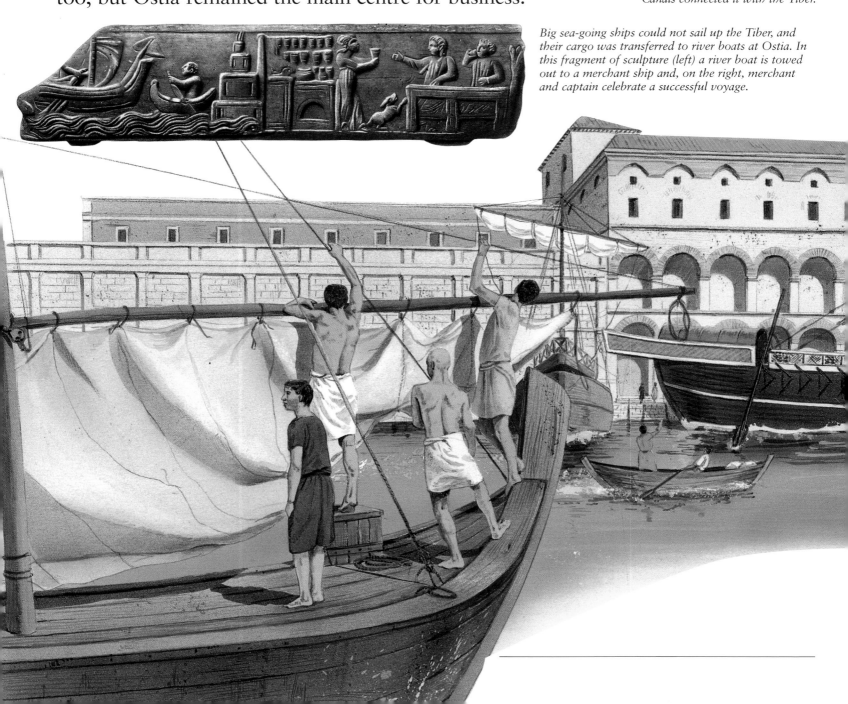

## Shipping

A typical merchant ship can be seen in the main picture below. It was made of wood with a rounded hull and a single mast set amidships. A square sail hung from a yard attached to the mast and the ship was steered with giant oars at the stern. Larger vessels might have two masts. Some big grain ships could carry up to 250 tons.

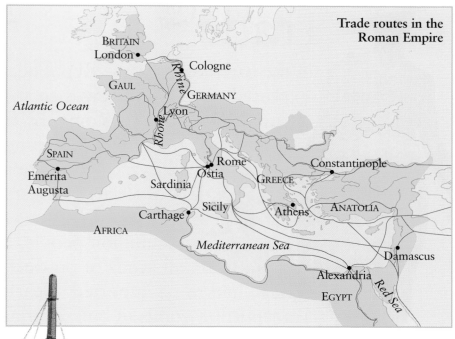

Trade routes in the Roman Empire

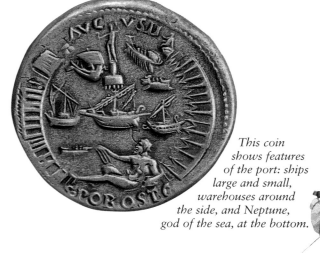

*This coin shows features of the port: ships large and small, warehouses around the side, and Neptune, god of the sea, at the bottom.*

## Trade routes

Trading ships crisscrossed the Mediterranean. They sailed as far as Britain for tin and other metals. The main rivers, such as the Rhine and the Rhone, were also busy trade routes. Roads were built for the army, but traders also used them.

*A busy scene in the port, with a cargo ship arriving, another behind preparing to leave, and the crew of a third (on the left) unfurling its sail. Behind are the warehouses, with a colonnade.*

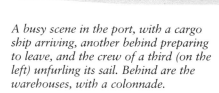

*Right: In the market, a female stallholder is selling fruit to a slave.*

# Trade

In the early years of the Republic, the Romans exported goods and grew their food in the country surrounding Rome. By the second century AD, they were importing almost everything, from all over the Empire and even beyond. Rome had no large industries or mass production, and everything was made by hand. To supply one million people, however poor most of them were, all kinds of products (from food and cloth to pots and pans) had to be imported. Nearly all this trade travelled by water. Transporting goods in bulk overland was slow and expensive. Rome's imports arrived by sea, then came up the River Tiber.

*Left: The fast-moving, winged Mercury, with his helmet and winged heels, was the god of traders. In this bronze he holds a purse of money. As messenger of the gods, he also carries his herald's staff.*

## Bankers

Roman banks were not like ours and played a smaller part in everyday life, but many banking services were available. A man could borrow money, though usually for a short time only and at high interest. He could make deposits, change currency (though Roman currency was accepted throughout the Empire), and operate on credit. Merchants borrowed money at interest to pay for cargo, because if the ship was wrecked the lender was the loser.

*Below: A banker checks his calculations. Rich landowners sometimes offered interest-free loans to friends or clients. Professional moneylenders charged high interest but they also took high risks.*

*The standard Roman coin was the silver denarius. There was a gold coin worth 25 denarii, and smaller coins in bronze or copper. Roman coinage came to dominate the Mediterranean region, but many local currencies existed in the different provinces, keeping money changers very busy.*

## Weights and measures

Gold and silver items were weighed on a simple balance, one half of which is shown above. Heavier objects were weighed on a steelyard. The object to be weighed was hung from a hook attached to a metal bar marked with a scale. A weight was moved along the bar until it was exactly horizontal. Then the weight could be read from the scale.

*Roman trade with China was irregular and small – only silk and some pottery like this dish (right). Goods travelled overland on the Silk Road, passing through many hands on the way.*

## Merchant shipping

Merchant ships varied from small coasters (above) to vessels carrying over 250 tons. They relied on square sails and oars, including steering oars (because they had no rudder). Merchants usually sailed their ships close to the coast, if they could, and preferred to spend nights in port. Shipwrecks were not uncommon (over 1,000 have been found by divers in recent years) and pirates were also a menace.

*Right: This beautiful glass amphora, with its stand, was found near the seaside town of Pompeii (which was buried by volcanic eruption in AD 79). Objects like this had to be imported, and were expensive.*

## Luxury trade

Wealthy people in the Roman Empire, although few in number compared with the masses of poor people, were extremely rich. They could afford Chinese silk, Indian jewels, rare perfumes, silver, fine glassware, works of art, and exotic foods. Julius Caesar banned excessive use of the expensive purple dye that came from Tyre. It was made from a type of shellfish, and tens of thousands of them were needed to make enough dye for just one toga.

*Left: This detail of a relief sculpture from southern Germany shows an oar-powered ship heavily laden with barrels of wine.*

## Exotic animals

Some traders made big profits by importing wild animals for the 'games'. In the emperor Trajan's games of AD 107, held to celebrate a recent victory, 11,000 animals were killed in a few weeks. This was big business. Lions, tigers, rhinoceroses, camels, crocodiles, bears, wolves, and even elephants were all shipped to Rome to die in the Colosseum for the entertainment of the people.

# Index